The Image of Christ

Art by Morgan Weistling

Baker Books

A Division of Baker Book House Co
Grand Rapids, Michigan 49516

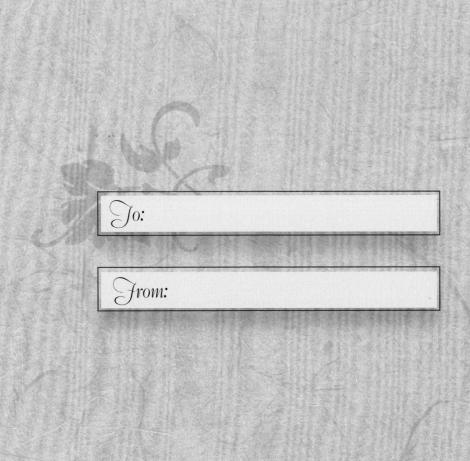

To:

From:

THE Image OF Christ

Art by Morgan Weistling

Baker Books

A Division of Baker Book House Co
Grand Rapids, Michigan 49516

For information about art prints by Morgan Weistling call Visions of Faith, 800-853-1352.

For current information about all releases from Baker Book House, visit our web site:

http://www.bakerbooks.com

_____

Cover and interior design by Brian Brunsting

Contents

Genesis 1:27

Introduction

Just as Christ revealed himself to us in human form more than two thousand years ago, his image is revealed today in the lives, the words, and the work of those who honor him.

As believers and followers of Christ, we wish to better know our Lord and Savior. Through this collection of art and poetry, let us celebrate the many ways in which he graciously makes himself known to us.

John 1:14

The Word became flesh and made his dwelling among us. We have seen his glory, the glory of the One and Only, who came from the Father, full of grace and truth.

Saviour, Breathe an Evening Blessing

Saviour, breathe an evening blessing,
Ere repose our spirits seal;
Sin and want we come confessing,
Thou canst save, and Thou canst heal.

Though the night be dark and dreary,
Darkness cannot hide from Thee;
Thou art He who, never weary,
Watchest where Thy people be.

Though destruction walk around us,
Though the arrow past us fly,
Angel-guards from Thee surround us,
We are safe if Thou art nigh.

Blessed Spirit, brooding o'er us,
Chase the darkness of our night,
Till the perfect day before us
Breaks in ever-lasting light.

James Edmeston, 1791–1867

The Reflection of God

Colossians 1:15–20 speaks of Christ's supremacy and of his being the image of the invisible God. Studying this passage brought the scene of Jesus' baptism to mind. God's voice came down from heaven, saying, "You are my son, whom I love; with you I am well pleased" (Mark 1:11).

I chose to depict a quiet moment while Jesus was in the Jordan River to be baptized by John. I wanted to focus on Christ alone, looking to his Father in heaven, as he fulfilled God's promise to send a Savior. His reflection in the water extends forward, reaching out to us, the viewers, as does Christ himself with his immeasurable gift of salvation.

My prayer is that this painting will not only proclaim the deity of Christ but will provoke the viewer to answer the question that Jesus asks all of us: "Who do you say I am?" (Matt. 16:15).

Morgan Weistling

13

To Jesus

Rise, O my soul, with thy desires to heaven,
And with divinest contemplation use
Thy time where time's eternity is given,
And let vain thoughts no more thy thoughts abuse;
But down in midnight darkness let them lie;
So live thy better, let thy worse thoughts die!

And thou, my soul, inspired with holy flame,
View and review with most regardful eye
That holy Cross, whence thy salvation came,
On which thy Saviour and thy sin did die!
For in that sacred object is much pleasure,
And in that Saviour is my life, my treasure.

To Thee, O Jesu! I direct my eye,
To Thee my hands, to Thee my humble knees;
To Thee my heart shall offer sacrifice;
To Thee my thoughts, Who my thoughts only sees:
To Thee myself, myself and all I give;
To Thee I die, to Thee I only live!

Sir Walter Raleigh, 1552–1618

14

From *Abt Vogler*

IX

Therefore to whom turn I but to thee, the ineffable Name?
    Builder and maker, thou, of houses not made with hands!
What, have fear of change from thee who art ever the same?
    Doubt that thy power can fill the heart that thy power expands?
There shall never be one lost good! What was, shall live as before;
    The evil is null, is naught, is silence implying sound;
What was good shall be good, with, for evil, so much good more;
    On the earth the broken arcs; in the heaven a perfect round.

X

All we have willed or hoped or dreamed of good shall exist;
    Not its semblance, but itself; no beauty, nor good, nor power
Whose voice has gone forth, but each survives for the melodist
    When eternity affirms the conception of an hour.
The high that proved too high, the heroic for earth too hard,
    The passion that left the ground to lose itself in the sky,
Are music sent up to God by the lover and the bard;
    Enough that he heard it once; we shall hear it by and by.

Robert Browning, 1812–1889

The Holy Spirit

Our blest Redeemer, ere He breathed
   His tender last farewell,
A Guide, a Comforter bequeathed,
   With us to dwell.

He came in tongues of living flame,
   To teach, convince, subdue;
All-powerful as the wind He came,
   As viewless too.

He came sweet influence to impart,
   A gracious, willing Guest,
While He can find one humble heart
   Wherein to rest.

And His that gentle voice we hear,
   Soft as the breath of even,
That checks each fault, that calms each fear,
   And speaks of heaven.

And every virtue we possess,
   And every victory won,
And every thought of holiness
   Are His alone.

Spirit of purity and grace,
   Our weakness pitying see;
O make our hearts Thy dwelling-place,
   And worthier Thee.

Harriet Auber, 1773–1862

Thy Will Be Done

This painting is a portrait of prayer. I was struck by the number of times the Bible refers to Christ going off alone and praying to his Father, such as in Luke 5:16: "But Jesus often withdrew to lonely places and prayed." This led me to paint Christ deep in prayer as he was so much of the time.

In this painting I wanted the viewer to imagine how Jesus would look if you were to come upon him in a private moment of prayer. I wanted to emphasize his strong carpenter's hands, clasped in prayer, representing his communion with the Father.

The title is from The Lord's Prayer, in which Christ taught us how we should pray to the Father. This painting is a gentle reminder to cling to God in prayer, not only in times of need but thoughtfully and often, just as Christ did.

Morgan Weistling

E.M. Bounds
on Prayer

God is vitally concerned that men should pray.
Men are bettered by prayer, and the world is bettered by praying. God does his best work for the
world through prayer. God's greatest glory and
man's highest good are secured by prayer. Prayer
forms the godliest men and makes the godliest
world.

E. M. Bounds, *The Complete Works
of E. M. Bounds,* page 238

He who dwells in the shelter

of the Most High

will rest in the shadow

of the Almighty.

I will say of the LORD,

"He is my refuge and my fortress,

my God, in whom I trust."

Psalm 91:1–2

Our Refuge and Our Strength

This painting depicts one of my favorite stories from the life of Christ. I remember reading about Jesus walking on the water and noting that he was out in the middle of the lake! This had a profound effect on me.

In this painting I wanted to give Peter's point of view, as though the viewer is struggling in the water with him. And like Peter, we come to the realization that Christ is there to save us, suggested by the light breaking through the turbulent clouds.

God is love; His mercy brightens
    All the path in which we rove;
Bliss He wakes and so He lightens:
    God is wisdom, God is love.

Chance and change are busy ever;
    Man decays and ages move;
But His mercy waneth never;
    God is wisdom, God is love.

Even the hour that darkest seemeth
    Will His changeless goodness prove;
From the mist His brightness streameth:
    God is wisdom, God is love.

He with earthly cares entwineth
    Hope and comfort from above:
Everywhere His glory shineth:
    God is wisdom, God is love.

John Bowring, 1792–1872

My Guide

There is no path in this desert waste;
    For the winds have swept the shifting sands,
The trail is blind where the storms have raced,
    And a stranger, I, in these fearsome lands.
But I journey on with a lightsome tread;
    I do not falter nor turn aside,
For I see His figure just ahead—
    He knows the way—my Guide.

There is no path in this trackless sea;
    No map is lined on the restless waves;
The ocean snares are strange to me
    Where the unseen wind in its fury raves.
But it matters naught; my sails are set,
    And my swift prow tosses the seas aside,
For the changeless stars are steadfast yet,
    And I sail by His star-blazed trail—my Guide.

There is no way in this starless night;
    There is naught but cloud in the inky skies;
The black night smothers me, left and right,
    I stare with a blind man's straining eyes.
But my steps are firm, for I cannot stray;
    The path to my feet seems light and wide;
For I hear His voice—"I am the way!"
    And I sing as I follow Him on—my Guide.

        Robert J. Burdette, 1844–1914

Jesus, Refuge of the Weary

Jesus, refuge of the weary,
Treasure of the spirit's love,
Fountain in life's desert dreary,
Saviour from the world above;
O how oft Thine eyes, offended,
Gaze upon the sinner's fall!
Yet upon the cross extended,
Thou didst bear the pain of all.

Do we pass that cross unheeding,
Breathing no repentant vow,
Though we see Thee, wounded, bleeding,
See Thy thorn-encircled brow!
Yet Thy sinless death has brought us
Life eternal, peace and rest;
Only what Thy grace has taught us
Calms the sinner's stormy breast.

Jesus, may our hearts be burning
With more fervent love for Thee!
May our eyes be ever turning
To Thy cross of agony;
Till in glory, parted never
From the blessed Saviour's side,
Graven in our hearts for ever,
Dwell the cross, the Crucified.

Girolamo Savonarola, 1452–1498

The Lilies of the Field

When I went up to Nazareth—
    A pilgrim of the spring—
When I went up to Nazareth
    The earth was blossoming!
I saw the blue flower of the flax
    Beside a shepherd's fold;
Along the hillsides' stony tracks
    I found the marigold;
The iris raised a shimmering spire
    Of beauty at my feet;
The poppy was a cup of fire
    Among the cooling wheat!

When I went up to Nazareth
    I marked how time came down
With blighting dust and withering breath
    Upon the hallowed town!
The years that buried Babylon
    Were drifting to efface
The steps of Mary's Heavenly Son,
    But still his truth held place,
And still I read his permanence
    By signs that never dim:
With all their ancient eloquence;
    The lilies spoke of him.

Daniel Henderson, b. 1880

Lilies of the Field

This scene emphasizes Christ's message that we shouldn't worry: "Consider how the lilies grow. . . . If that is how God clothes the grass of the field . . . how much more will he clothe you" (Luke 12:27–28). Worrying is a daily tendency for me, so I find this passage especially comforting.

Just consider the intricate detail found in all of creation and how the Lord has provided for the needs of plants and animals. Yet plants and animals are not as precious as the life he has given us. It is senseless to think that he wouldn't take care of our needs.

In my painting, Christ stands with his arms open and invites us to the peace that only he can give. He said, "Come to me, all you who are weary and burdened, and I will give you rest" (Matt. 11:29).

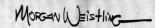

25

Consider the

He hides within the lily
    A strong and tender Care,
That wins the earth-born atoms
    To glory of the air;
He weaves the shining garments
    Unceasingly and still,
Along the quiet waters,
    In niches of the hill.

We linger at the vigil
    With him who bent the knee,
To watch the old-time lilies
    In distant Galilee;
And still the worship deepens
    And quickens into new,
As brightening down the ages
    God's secret thrilleth through.

Lilies

O Toiler of the lily,
    Thy touch is in the man!
No leaf that dawns to petal
    But hints the angel-plan:
The flower-horizons open,
    The blossom vaster shows;
We hear thy wide world's echo,—
    "See how the lily grows!"

Shy yearnings of the savage,
    Unfolding, thought by thought,
To holy lives are lifted,
    To visions fair are wrought:
The races rise and cluster,
    And evils fade and fall,
Till chaos blooms to beauty,
    Thy purpose crowning all!

William Channing Gannett, 1840–1923

Jesus

From "The Testament of Beauty"

So it was when Jesus came in his gentleness
with his divine compassion and great Gospel of Peace,
men hail'd him WORD OF GOD, and in the title of Christ
crown'd him with love beyond all earth-names of renown.
For He, wandering unarm'd save by the Spirit's flame,
in few years with few friends founded a world-empire
wider than Alexander's and more enduring;
since from his death it took its everlasting life.
HIS kingdom is God's kingdom, and his holy temple
not in Athens or Rome but in the heart of man.
They who understand not cannot forget, and they
who keep not his commandment call him Master and Lord.

Robert Bridges, 1844–1930

Kissing the Face of God

This painting was inspired by a song that I heard one day. The phrase "kissing the face of God" immediately struck me with this powerful image of Mary and baby Jesus.

I started to contemplate the awesome privilege that Mary was given, being able to hold God in her arms. At the same time he was still her baby. This cute little child whom she bore was also God in the flesh, and yet she cuddled and kissed him, just as all mothers do with their babies. This thought propelled me right into this painting, which I wanted to be a human representation of divinity.

My prayer is that the viewer will be struck, as I am, with the amazing way that God chose to send his Son into this world—in pure humility.

Morgan Weistling

29

The King Eternal

Hail to the Lord's Anointed,
   Great David's greater Son!
Hail, in the time appointed,
   His reign on earth begun!
He comes to break oppression,
   To set the captive free,
To take away transgression,
   And rule in equity.

He comes with succour speedy
   To those who suffer wrong,
To help the poor and needy,
   And bid the weak be strong,

To give them songs for sighing,
   Their darkness turn to light
Whose souls, condemned and dying,
   Were precious in His sight.
He shall come down like showers
   Upon the fruitful earth;
And love, joy, hope, like flowers
   Spring in His path to birth.
Before Him, on the mountains,
   Shall peace, the herald, go;
And righteousness, in fountains,
   From hill to valley flow.

Kings shall fall down before Him,
    And gold and incense bring;
All nations shall adore Him,
    His praise all people sing:
For He shall have dominion
    O'er river, sea, and shore,
Far as the eagle's pinion
    Or dove's light wing can soar.

For Him shall prayer unceasing
    And daily vows ascend;
His Kingdom still increasing,
    A Kingdom without end:
The mountain dews shall nourish
    A seed in weakness sown,
Whose fruit shall spread and flourish,
    And shake like Lebanon.

O'er every foe victorious,
    He on His throne shall rest,
From age to age more glorious,
    All blessing and all-blest.
The tide of time shall never
    His covenant remove;
His Name shall stand for ever;
    That Name to us is Love.

James Montgomery, 1771–1854

Crucifixion

This is my attempt to capture the most painful moment in Christ's life, when the Father withdrew from him so he could die and take the punishment for our sins. The light shining in his eyes is about to fade into darkness, as Christ goes through this experience truly alone.

I pray that every time the viewer sees this painting it will be a reminder of how Christ saved us from ever having to experience this. "God demonstrates his own love for us in this: While we were still sinners, Christ died for us" (Rom. 5:8).

In the Cross
of Christ I Glory

In the cross of Christ I glory,
Towering o'er the wrecks of time;
All the light of sacred story
Gathers round its head sublime.

When the woes of life o'er take me,
Hopes deceive, and fears annoy,
Never shall the cross forsake me:
Lo! it glows with peace and joy.

When the sun of bliss is beaming
Light and love upon my way,
From the cross the radiance streaming
Adds more luster to the day.

Bane and blessing, pain and pleasure,
By the cross are sanctified;
Peace is there that knows no measure,
Joys that through all time abide.

In the cross of Christ I glory,
Towering o'er the wrecks of time;
All the light of sacred story
Gathers round its head sublime.

John Bowring, 1792–1872

Then he said, "Jesus,

remember me when you come

into your kingdom."

Jesus answered him, "I tell you

the truth, today you will

be with me in paradise."

Luke 23:42–43

The story of the salvation of the dying thief is a standing instance of the power of Christ to save, and of His abundant willingness to receive all that come to Him, in whatever plight they might be. I cannot regard this act of grace as a solitary instance, any more than the salvation of Zacchæus, the restoration of Peter, or the call of Saul, the persecutor. Every conversion is, in a sense, singular: no two are exactly alike, and yet any one conversion is a type of others. The case of the dying thief is much more similar to our conversion than it is dissimilar; in point of fact, his case may be regarded as typical, rather than as an extraordinary incident.

Charles H. Spurgeon, *Christ's Words from the Cross*, page 31

Walking with God

When Jesus was growing up it must have been incredible for Joseph to know that the Son of God was entrusted to him to raise. As I contemplated this thought, I saw this scene when Jesus took his first steps on earth.

Here, in Joseph's carpenter shop, Jesus is being helped by Joseph. Yet the irony is that Jesus' last footsteps on earth would lead him to a wooden cross that would save all who believe, including Joseph.

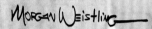

Love Divine, all loves excelling,
Joy of heaven, to earth come down,
Fix in us Thy humble dwelling,
All Thy faithful mercies crown.
Jesus, Thou art all compassion;
Pure, unbounded love Thou art;
Visit us with Thy salvation,
Enter every trembling heart.

Come, Almighty to deliver;
Let us all Thy grace receive;
Suddenly return, and never,
Never more Thy temples leave.
Thee we would be always blessing,
Serve Thee as Thy hosts above,
Pray, and praise Thee, without ceasing,
Glory in Thy perfect love.

Finish, then, Thy new creation;
Pure and spotless let us be;
Let us see Thy great salvation,
Perfectly restored in Thee,
Changed from glory into glory,
Till in heaven we take our place,
Till we cast our crowns before Thee,
Lost in wonder, love, and praise.

Charles Wesley, 1707–1788

God Within Yet Above

The peaks, and the starlit skies, the deeps of the fathomless seas,
Immanent is He in all, yet higher and deeper than these.

The heart, and the mind, and the soul, the thoughts
    and the yearnings of Man,
Of His essence are one and all, and yet define it who can?

The love of the Right, tho' cast down, the hate of victorious ill,
All are sparks from the central fire of a boundless beneficent Will.

Oh, mystical secrets of Nature, great Universe undefined,
Ye are parts of the infinite work of a mighty ineffable Mind.

Beyond your limitless Space, before your measureless Time,
Ere Life or Death began was this changeless Essence sublime.

In the core of eternal calm He dwelleth unmoved and alone
Mid the Universe He has made, as a monarch upon his throne.

And the self-same inscrutable Power which fashioned the sun and the star
Is Lord of the feeble strength of the humblest creatures that are.

The weak things that float or creep for their little life of a day,
The weak souls that falter and faint, as feeble and futile as they;

The malefic invisible atoms unmarked by man's purblind eye
That beleaguer our House of Life, and compass us till we die;

All these are parts of Him, the indivisible One,
Who supports and illumines the many, Creation's Pillar and Sun!

Yea, and far in the depths of Being, too dark for a mortal brain,
Lurk His secrets of Evil and Wrong, His creatures of Death and Pain.

A viewless Necessity binds, a determinate Impetus drives
To a hidden invisible goal the freightage of numberless lives.

The waste, and the pain, and the wrong, the abysmal mysteries dim,
Come not of themselves alone, but are seed and issue of Him.

And Man's spirit that spends and is spent in mystical questionings,
Oh, the depths of the fathomless deep, oh, the riddle and secret of things,
And the voice through the darkness heard, and the rush of winnowing wings!

Lewis Morris, 1833–1907

Healing the Blind Man

In this painting I portray the reactions of people to Christ's miracles. When he would perform a miracle such as this one, spitting on the ground to make mud to heal the blind man, the Pharisees would make plans to kill him. It amazes me that some would be in disbelief, even though they saw the miracles, and others would fall at the feet of the living God.

Today people's reactions are much the same to Jesus and the work he continues to do through his church.

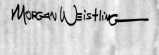

"I believe it! 'Tis thou, God, that givest, 'tis I who receive:
In the first is the last, in thy will is my power to believe.
All's one gift: thou canst grant it moreover, as prompt to my prayer
As I breathe out this breath, as I open these arms to the air.
From thy will stream the worlds, life and nature, thy dread Sabaoth:
I will?—the mere atoms despise me! Why am I not loth
To look that, even that in the face too? Why is it I dare
Think but lightly of such impuissance? What stops my despair?
This;—'tis not what man Does which exalts him, but what man Would do!
See the King—I would help him but cannot, the wishes fall through.
Could I wrestle to raise him from sorrow, grow poor to enrich,
To fill up his life, starve my own out, I would—knowing which,
I know that my service is perfect. Oh, speak through me now!
Would I suffer for him that I love? So wouldst thou—so wilt thou!
So shall crown thee the topmost, ineffablest, uttermost crown—
And thy love fill infinitude wholly, nor leave up nor down
One spot for the creature to stand in! It is by no breath,
Turn of eye, wave of hand, that salvation joins issue with death!
As thy Love is discovered almighty, almighty be proved
Thy power, that exists with and for it, of being Beloved!
He who did most, shall bear most; the strongest shall stand the most weak.
'Tis the weakness in strength, that I cry for! my flesh, that I seek
In the Godhead! I seek and I find it. O Saul, it shall be
A Face like my face that receives thee; a Man like to me,
Thou shalt love and be loved by, forever: a Hand like this hand
Shall throw open the gates of new life to thee! See the Christ stand!"

Robert Browning, 1812–1889

Kinsman

And didst Thou love the race that loved not Thee?
    And didst Thou take to heaven a human brow?
Dost plead with man's voice by the marvellous sea?
    Art Thou his Kinsman now?

O God, O Kinsman loved, but not enough,
    O Man, with eyes majestic after death,
Whose feet have toiled along our pathways rough,
    Whose lips drawn human breath!—

By that one likeness which is ours and Thine,
    By that one nature which doth hold us kin,
By that high heaven where, sinless, Thou dost shine
    To draw us sinners in;

By Thy last silence in the judgment hall,
    By long foreknowledge of the deadly Tree,
By darkness, by the wormwood and the gall,
    I pray Thee visit me.

Come, lest this heart should, cold and cast away,
    Die ere the Guest adored she entertain—
Lest eyes which never saw Thine earthly day
    Should miss Thy heavenly reign.

Jean Ingelow, 1820–1897

God's Mercy

There's a wideness in God's mercy,
    Like the wideness of the sea;
There's a kindness in His justice
    Which is more than liberty.

There is no place where earth's sorrows
    Are more felt than up in heaven;
There is no place where earth's failings
    Have such kindly judgment given.

For the love of God is broader
    Than the measure of man's mind,
And the heart of the Eternal
    Is most wonderfully kind.

If our love were but more simple,.
    We should take Him at His word,
And our lives would be all sunshine
    In the sweetness of our Lord.

Frederick William Faber, 1814–1863

Jesus of the Scars

If we have never sought, we seek Thee now;
    Thine eyes burn through the dark, our only stars;
We must have sight of thorn-pricks on Thy brow,
    We must have Thee, O Jesus of the Scars.

The heavens frighten us; they are too calm;
    In all the universe we have no place.
Our wounds are hurting us; where is the balm?
    Lord Jesus, by Thy Scars we claim Thy grace.

If when the doors are shut, Thou drawest near,
    Only reveal those hands, that side of Thine;
We know to-day what wounds are, have no fear,
    Show us Thy Scars, we know the countersign.

The other gods were strong; but Thou wast weak;
    They rode, but Thou didst stumble to a throne;
But to our wounds only God's wounds can speak,
    And not a god has wounds, but Thou alone.

Edward Shillito, 1872–1948

Known by His Scars

We don't know what Jesus looks like, yet when we come face-to-face with him some-day, we will recognize him by his scars. I painted Christ's face in shadows to show how unimportant his facial features really are. I focused instead on the markings that built a bridge between man and God.

Christ's scars represent his suffering and death for the forgiveness of all of humankind's sins. John the Baptist said about Jesus, "Look, the Lamb of God, who takes away the sin of the world!" (John 1:29).

As the resurrected and living Christ shows us his scars from the wounds he endured out of love for us, he also stands before us and offers his love to all who will accept him.

Morgan Weistling

I have been crucified

with Christ and I

no longer live,

but Christ lives in me.

The life I live in the body,

I live by faith in the Son of God,

who loved me

and gave himself for me.

Galatians 2:20

There can be no greater need than to know that our God is no stranger to pain. He is, as Henri Nouwen pointed out, the wounded healer. To each inquisitor who wants to know where our Messiah can be found, we must say again, "He is outside the city near the gates. He sits bandaged, yet he invites all those who are injured to come to him for healing." He does not heal by waving a magic wand above the hurting. Nor does he traffic in prayer cloths. His healing power derives from his own pain, from having iron spikes driven through his body. With that ugly triumph he can heal.

When Pilate asked Jesus, "What is truth?" his question went unanswered—at least Christ gave him no verbal answer. Jesus' silence may have come because he realized that Pilate was really asking, "Why am I upon this planet?" . . .

Pilate must have ached over his own lack of inner meaning when he saw Jesus affirming his kingship on the brink of death. He must have envied Jesus' confidence at knowing why he was on the planet, at seeing great purpose in the death he must endure. Jesus was silent, not because he didn't know the answer to Pilate's question, but because he knew the answer could only be revealed by dying. It could not be revealed by mere words.

Calvin Miller, *Once upon a Tree*, pages 159, 15–16

Salutation to Jesus Christ

I greet thee, my Redeemer sure,
    I trust in none but thee,
Thou who hast borne such toil and shame
    And suffering for me:
Our hearts from cares and cravings vain
    And foolish fears set free.

Thou art the King compassionate,
    Thou reignest everywhere,
Almighty Lord, reign thou in us,
    Rule all we have and are:
Enlighten us and rise to heaven,
    Amid thy glories there.

Thou art the life by which we live;
    Our stay and strength's in thee;
Uphold us so in face of death,
    What time soe'er it be,
That we may meet it with strong heart,
    And may die peacefully.

Our hope is in none else but thee;
    Faith holds thy promise fast;
Be pleased, Lord, to strengthen us,
    Whom Thou redeemed hast,
To bear all troubles patiently,
    And overcome at last. . . .

John Calvin, 1509–1564

The King of Love

The King of love my Shepherd is,
    Whose goodness faileth never;
I nothing lack if I am His,
    And He is mine forever.

Where streams of living water flow
    My ransomed soul He leadeth,
And where the verdant pastures grow
    With food celestial feedeth.

Perverse and foolish oft I strayed,
    But yet in love He sought me,
And on His shoulder gently laid,
    And home rejoicing brought me.

In death's dark vale I fear no ill,
    With Thee, dear Lord, beside me;
Thy rod and staff my comfort still,
    Thy cross before to guide me.

Thou spread'st a table in my sight;
    Thy unction grace bestoweth;
And O what transport of delight
    From Thy pure chalice floweth.

And so, through all the length of day,
    Thy goodness faileth never;
Good Shepherd, may I sing Thy praise
    Within Thy house forever.

Henry W. Baker, 1821–1877

The Lord Is My Shepherd

Often, in Scripture, we find the analogy of our Lord as a Shepherd and we, the faithful, as his flock.

In Luke 15:3–7, Jesus' parable of the lost sheep, we find the Good Shepherd going out and looking for one lost sheep, rejoicing when he finds it, and putting it on his shoulders to bring it home.

I see myself on those shoulders, as Christ carries me through life. I was lost, and now I am found by the Good Shepherd who loves me. I pray that you will see yourself on those strong shoulders, knowing that our Shepherd laid down his life for us, his sheep who have gone astray.

Morgan Weistling

My Lord and My God

After Jesus' resurrection, he came to his disciples, but Thomas still did not believe it was him. "Then he said to Thomas, 'Put your finger here; see my hands. Reach out your hand and put it into my side. Stop doubting and believe.' Thomas said to him, 'My Lord and my God!'" (John 20:27–28).

Thomas testified to the truth of Jesus' divinity, and Jesus did not rebuke him, but rather commended those who would believe this truth without seeing for themselves.

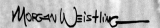

I Think
When I Read
That Sweet Story of Old

I think, when I read that sweet story of old,
    When Jesus was here among men,
How He called little children as lambs to His fold,
    I should like to have been with them then;
I wish that His hands had been placed on my head,
    That His arms had been thrown around me,
And that I might have seen His kind look when He said,
    "Let the little ones come unto Me."

Yet still to His footstool in prayer I may go,
    And ask for a share in His love;
And, if I now earnestly seek Him below,
    I shall see Him and hear Him above,
In that beautiful place He is gone to prepare
    For all who are washed and forgiven;
And many dear children are gathering there,
    For of such is the Kingdom of heaven.

But thousands and thousands, who wander and fall,
    Never heard of that heavenly home;
I should like them to know there is room for them all,
    And that Jesus has bid them to come.
I long for the joy of that glorious time,
    The sweetest and brightest and best,
When the dear little children of every clime
    Shall crowd to His arms and be blest.

Jemima Luke, 1813–1906

The Way, the Truth and the Life

O Thou great Friend to all the sons of men,
    Who once appeared in humblest guise below,
Sin to rebuke, to break the captive's chain,
    And call thy brethren forth from want and woe,—

We look to thee! thy truth is still the Light
    Which guides the nations, groping on their way,
Stumbling and falling in disastrous night,
    Yet hoping ever for the perfect day.

Yes; thou art still the Life, thou art the Way
    The holiest know; Light, Life, the Way of heaven!
And they who dearest hope and deepest pray,
    Toil by the Light, Life, Way, which thou hast given.

Theodore Parker, 1810–1860

The *Illimitable God*

From "A Death in the Desert," conclusion

If Christ, as thou affirmest, be of men
Mere man, the first and best but nothing more—
Account Him, for reward of what He was,
Now and for ever, wretchedest of all.
For see; Himself conceived of life as love,
Conceived of love as what must enter in,
Fill up, make one with His each soul He loved:
Thus much for man's joy, all men's joy for Him.
Well, He is gone, thou sayest, to fit reward.
But by this time are many souls set free,
And very many still retained alive:
Nay, should His coming be delayed awhile,
Say, ten years longer (twelve years some compute),
See if, for every finger of thy hands,
There be not found, that day the world shall end,
Hundreds of souls, each holding by Christ's word
That He will grow incorporate with all,
With me as Pamphylax, with him as John,
Groom for each bride! Can a mere man do this?
Yet Christ saith this He lived and died to do.
Call Christ, then, the illimitable God,
Or lost!

Robert Browning, 1812–1889

Genesis 1:27

So God created man
in his own image,
in the image of God
he created him;
male and female
he created them.

1. Christ speaks:

"My son,
I came down from heaven
to save you;
I willingly experienced hard things,
   not because I had to,
   but because I love you,
     so that you would learn
     patience,
   so that you would bear
   hard things ungrudgingly.
From the hour of My birth
to My death on the cross,
   I did not live without
   suffering grief.
     I suffered
       lack of everyday amenities,
       complaints against Me,
       disgraces and aspersions,
       ingratitude for blessings I gave,
       blasphemies for miracles,
       reproofs for teachings."

The Blacksmith

I love to watch a blacksmith forge something useful or beautiful from a rod of iron with just fire and a hammer. God shapes his children much the same way. The trials of life are sometimes the very things that God uses to shape us into what he desires us to be.

Morgan Weistling

2. I reply:

"That You lived patiently,
and therefore fulfilled Your Father's
command,
   is reason for me,
   a sinner,
   to bear hard things patiently,
   for this is Your will;
   and this will strengthen my soul—
      enduring the burden of this
      uncertain life
      so long as You choose to keep me alive.
         For, though this life
         is emotionally taxing,
         it is very profitable by Your
         grace;
         and because of Your example
         and the footsteps of the saints,
            life is brighter
            and more tolerable
            to the weak.
      Moreover, life has more
      consolation
      than it did under the old law,
         when heaven's gate was
         shut,
         and when the way to heaven
         seemed so obscure—
         when only a few
         took care
         to seek the
         kingdom of heaven.
         More, the saved
         could not enter the
         heavenly kingdom
            before the cross
            and atonement."

3. I say more:

"I must thank You,
You who promise to
show me
and all faithful people
   the right way to
   Your eternal kingdom.
      Your life is
      our way;
      by holy patience
      we walk in Your
      direction—
         You are our
         crown.
If you had not gone
ahead of us,
and taught us,
   who could have
   followed?
   Your example paved
   the way!
      Yet! we are lukewarm,
      even though we know about
         Your miracles and
         Your teachings.
      What would become of us
      if we didn't have
         You, our great light,
         to follow?"

Thomas à Kempis, *The Imitation of Christ*

Teach us to number our days aright,

that we may gain a heart of wisdom.

May the favor of the Lord our God

rest upon us; establish the work

of our hands for us—yes, establish

the work of our hands.

Psalm 90:12, 17

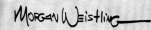

A Thankful Heart

I chose to portray this moment of prayer with a humble little meal rather than a sumptuous feast because we are to be thankful for the little we receive as well as the bounty.

The Bible urges, "Be joyful always; pray continually; give thanks in all circumstances, for this is God's will for you in Christ Jesus" (1 Thess. 5:16–18)

This may sound like a big order from God, asking us to be thankful for everything, but when you understand how much he loves us, how much he showed that love on the cross, and how little we deserve that love, thankfulness comes naturally.

Morgan Weistling

"With Whom Is No Variableness, Neither Shadow of Turning"

It fortifies my soul to know
That, though I perish, truth is so:
That, howsoe'er I stray and range,
Whate'er I do, Thou dost not change.
I steadier step when I recall
That, if I slip, Thou dost not fall.

Arthur Hugh Clough, 1819–1861

To Serve God
and Forsake the World

1. Lord Jesus,
   I want to speak to You again
   (I cannot keep still),
   I want to say this to you:
      My God and king in heaven,
      how great and abundant the sweetness
      You hide in reserve
         for those who honor You!
         To those who serve and love You wholeheartedly
         —unspeakably wonderful is the taste!
         And You really give this sweetness
         to those who love You.
   You proved this to me, Lord:
      When I was nothing,
        You made me something;
      when I turned far away from You,
        You brought me back again
          to serve You and
            made me love You. . . .

5. Serving You is a great honor
        a great glory;
serving You instead of the world
opens the door to Your magnanimous grace
   —that's the gift You present
   to those who freely submit to You—
      Your love for giving up carnal delights!
      Sweet-tasting consolations from the Holy Spirit!
      Great freedom of spirit for taking the narrow way!

6. Glad, delightful service to God!
This is the secret to freedom,
        to holy living.
This makes one equal to angels,
      pleasing to God,
      frightening to demons,
      honored by God's faithful people.
O welcome service,
   always desired,
     and for which God rewards
     us with highest goodness and
       eternal joy!

Thomas à Kempis, *The Imitation of Christ*

Our Burden Bearer

The little sharp vexations
    And the briars that cut the feet,
Why not take all to the Helper
    Who has never failed us yet?
Tell Him about the heartache,
    And tell Him the longings too,
Tell Him the baffled purpose
    When we scarce know what to do.
Then, leaving all our weakness
    With the One divinely strong,
Forget that we bore the burden
    And carry away the song.

Phillips Brooks, 1835–1893

Sisters

The love between these two sisters is self-evident and was true with my models, who are very close sisters in real life. Sometimes our best friends in life are our siblings, and this painting is a testimony to the love and caring possible in our families.

When we enter into God's family of believers, we also gain many more brothers and sisters in Christ. May we embrace our spiritual family and remember that we are all children of God in Christ.

Morgan Weistling

The Greatness of Love

1 Corinthians 13

I may speak with the tongues of men and of angels, but if I have no love,
   I am a noisy gong or a clanging cymbal;
I may prophesy, fathom all mysteries and secret lore,
I may have such absolute faith that I can move hills from their place,
   but if I have no love,
   I count for nothing;
I may distribute all I possess in charity,
I may give up my body to be burnt,
   but if I have no love,
   I make nothing of it.
Love is very patient, very kind
Love knows no jealousy;
Love makes no parade, gives itself no airs, is never rude, never selfish,
   never irritated, never resentful;
Love is never glad when others go wrong,
Love is gladdened by goodness, always slow to expose,
   always eager to believe the best, always hopeful, always patient.

Love never disappears.
As for prophesying, it will be superseded;
As for "tongues" they will cease;
As for knowledge, it will be superseded.
For we only know bit by bit, and we only prophesy bit by bit;
But when the perfect comes, the imperfect will be superseded.
When I was a child,
    I talked like a child,
    I thought like a child,
    I argued like a child;
Now that I am a man, I am done with childish ways.
At present we only see the baffling reflections in a mirror,
    but then it will be face to face;
At present I am learning bit by bit,
    But then I shall understand, as all along I have myself been understood.
Thus 'faith and hope and love last on, these three,'
    but the greatest of all is love.

Saint Paul, 1st century A.D.
The New Testament, A New Translation by James Moffatt, 1922

When Jesus walked this earth, the lonely and the destitute flocked to him. If Jesus were to have started his ministry today, Lonesome Joe would have been one of those whom Jesus would have ministered to.

As his church we are his body on earth. It is our responsibility to let Christ touch the lost and searching through us.

Morgan Weistling

Cast Your Cares on *God*

From "Enoch Arden" (L. 222)

Cast all your cares on God; that anchor holds.
Is He not yonder in those uttermost
Parts of the morning? If I flee to these,
Can I go from Him? And the sea is His,
The sea is His; He made it.

Alfred, Lord Tennyson, 1809–1892

Out in the Fields with God

The little cares that fretted me,
    I lost them yesterday,
Among the fields above the sea,
    Among the winds at play,
Among the lowing of the herds,
    The rustling of the trees,
Among the singing of the birds,
    The humming of the bees.

The foolish fears of what might pass
    I cast them all away
Among the clover-scented grass
    Among the new-mown hay,
Among the rustling of the corn
    Where drowsy poppies nod,
Where ill thoughts die and good are born—
    Out in the fields with God!

Author unknown

Eventide

At cool of day, with God I walk
    My garden's grateful shade;
I hear His voice among the trees,
    And I am not afraid.

He speaks to me in every wind,
    He smiles from every star;
He is not deaf to me, nor blind,
    Nor absent, nor afar.

His hand that shuts the flowers to sleep,
    Each in its dewy fold,
Is strong my feeble life to keep,
    And competent to hold.

The powers below and powers above,
    Are subject to His care—
I cannot wander from His love
    Who loves me everywhere.

Caroline Atherton Mason, 1823–1890

everywhere

Morgan Weistling

[Jesus] said,

"I am the light of the world.

Whoever follows me

will never walk in darkness,

but will have the light of life."

John 8:12

Faith

I will not doubt, though all my ships at sea
    Come drifting home with broken masts and sails;
    I shall believe the Hand which never fails,
From seeming evil worketh good to me;
    And, though I weep because those sails are battered,
    Still will I cry, while my best hopes lie shattered,
        "I trust in Thee."

I will not doubt, though all my prayers return
    Unanswered from the still, white realm above;
    I shall believe it is an all-wise Love
Which has refused those things for which I yearn;
    And though, at times, I cannot keep from grieving,
    Yet the pure ardor of my fixed believing
        Undimmed shall burn.

I will not doubt, though sorrows fall like rain,
      And troubles swarm like bees about a hive;
      I shall believe the heights for which I strive,
Are only reached by anguish and by pain;
      And, though I groan and tremble with my crosses,
      I yet shall see, through my severest losses,
            The greater gain.

I will not doubt; well anchored in the faith,
      Like some stanch ship, my soul braves every gale,
      So strong its courage that it will not fail
To breast the mighty, unknown sea of death.
      Oh, may I cry when body parts with spirit,
      "I do not doubt," so listening worlds may hear it
            With my last breath.

Ella Wheeler Wilcox, 1855–1919

Graces

This young girl exemplifies the concept of graces, both physically and spiritually. There is an air of elegance about her, but even more striking is the light that she radiates from within. Her whole demeanor exudes a sense of kindness and benevolence; characteristics that will distinguish her throughout her life.

As she posed in the sunlight, she reminded me of 2 Peter 3:18: "Grow in the grace and knowledge of our Lord and Savior Jesus Christ. To him be the glory both now and forever!"

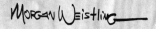

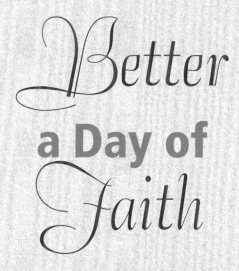

Better a Day of Faith

Better a day of faith
Than a thousand years of doubt!
Better one mortal hour with Thee
Than an endless life without!

Thou art a mighty Wall,
Skirting life's darkened stair;
Groping my way alone,
Lo, I have found Thee there!

Henry Burke Robins, b. 1874

At Even, When the Sun Was Set

At even, when the sun was set,
   The sick O Lord, around Thee lay;
O in what divers pains they met!
   O with what joy they went away!

Once more 'tis eventide, and we,
   Oppressed with various ills, draw near;
What if Thy form we cannot see,
   We know and feel that Thou art here.

O Saviour Christ, our woes dispel;
   For some are sick, and some are sad,
And some have never loved Thee well,
   And some have lost the love they had;

And some are pressed with worldly care,
   And some are tried with sinful doubt;
And some such grievous passions tear,
   That only Thou canst cast them out;

And some have found the world is vain,
    Yet from the world they break not free;
And some have friends who give them pain,
    Yet have not sought a Friend in Thee;

And none, O Lord, have perfect rest,
    For none are wholly free from sin;
And they who fain would serve Thee best
    Are conscious most of wrong within.

O Saviour Christ, Thou too art Man;
    Thou hast been troubled, tempted, tried;
Thy kind but searching glance can scan
    The very wounds that shame would hide;

Thy touch has still its ancient power;
    No word from Thee can fruitless fall;
Hear, in this solemn evening hour,
    And in Thy mercy heal us all.

Henry Twells, 1823–1900

Inconstancy

1. My son,
     don't trust your feelings;
          they say one thing now,
          but another in no time at all.
     You are subject to changing moods
     so long as you're alive,
     even when you don't want mood changes:
          now you feel merry-hearted,
          then you turn sad;
          another time you are peaceful,
          next you are troubled in spirit;
          one moment you feel devout,
          another unspiritual;
          now you are diligent,
          next listless;
          you are sober,
          then lighthearted.
     But wise people,
          well-instructed in the Spirit,
          stand fast during mood changes,
          paying no attention to feelings,
          ignoring which way the wind of instability blows,
               focusing the whole
               intent of the mind
               on right and best
               goals.
                    This way one stays the same,
                    unshaken
                    in the welter of events,
                    consistently looking to Me
                    with a single eye.

2. The purer the eye of intent,
   the greater the stability
      in any kind of storm
      that assails one.
         But in many,
         the eye of intent
         goes dim
            because
            deceptively pleasurable
            stimuli
            catch its gaze.
               Rare is the person
               really free
               of the blemish called
               self-seeking.
                     So people came to Bethany,
                        not only to see Martha and Mary,
                        not only to see Jesus,
                           but to see Lazarus, too.

The eye of intent, therefore,
must be purified
   to make us single-hearted,
   rightly motivated, and
   Christ-oriented,
      to enable us
      to live beyond
         eye-catching stimuli
         that can come
         between us and God.

Thomas à Kempis, *The Imitation of Christ*

Lord, Come Away!

Lord, come away;
　　Why dost Thou stay?
Thy road is ready and Thy paths made straight
With longing expectation wait
The consecration of Thy beauteous feet.
Ride on triumphantly: behold! we lay
Our lusts and proud wills in Thy way.
Hosannah! welcome to our hearts: Lord, here
Thou hast a temple too, and full as dear
As that of Sion; and as full of sin—
Nothing but thieves and robbers dwell therein;
Enter, and chase them forth, and cleanse the floor,
Crucify them, that they may never more
　　Profane that holy place
　　Where Thou hast chose to set Thy face.
And then if our still tongues shall be
Mute in the praises of Thy deity,
　　The stones out of the temple wall
　　Shall cry aloud and call
Hosannah! and Thy glorious footsteps greet.

Jeremy Taylor, 1613–1667

I Heard the Voice of Jesus

I heard the voice of Jesus say,
"Come unto Me and rest;
Lay down, thou weary one, lay down
Thy head upon my breast:"
I came to Jesus as I was,
Weary, and worn, and sad;
I found in Him a resting-place,
And He has made me glad.

I heard the voice of Jesus say,
"Behold, I freely give
The living water, thirsty one,
Stoop down, and drink, and live:"
I came to Jesus, and I drank
Of that life-giving stream;
My thirst was quench'd, my soul revived,
And now I live in Him.

I heard the voice of Jesus say,
"I am this dark world's light;
Look unto Me, thy morn shall rise,
And all thy day be bright:"
I look'd to Jesus, and I found
In Him my star, my sun;
And in that light of life I'll walk
Till travelling days are done.

Horatius Bonar, 1808–1889

I Will Not Hurry

I will not hurry through this day!
Lord, I will listen by the way,
To humming bees and singing birds,
To speaking trees and friendly words;
And for the moments in between
Seek glimpses of Thy great Unseen.

I will not hurry through this day;
I will take time to think and pray;
I will look up into the sky,
Where fleecy clouds and swallows fly;
And somewhere in the day, maybe
I will catch whispers, Lord, from Thee!

Ralph Spaulding Cushman, b. 1879

Now we see

but a poor reflection

as in a mirror;

then we shall see face to face.

Now I know in part;

then I shall know fully,

even as I am fully known.

1 Corinthians 13:12

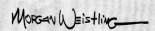

Index of Poems

and Prose

Index of Poets

and Authors

Scripture Index

Morgan Weistling enjoyed a notable career in the entertainment industry, designing movie posters and originating art for collector plates, pinball machines, and covers for magazines, books, CDs, and video games. Adding a new and important dimension to his work, Weistling now paints images that reflect his faith. He lives with his family in California.